Deeply in love, Edward, Duke of Kent, and Katharine Worsley had to wait six long years to prove the strength of their feelings. But theirs was to be a happy and enduring marriage despite the tragedies of miscarriage and Katharine's mental anguish.

Baron/Camera Press

DEVOTED FAMILIES

YOUNG EDWARD OF KENT'S LIFE WAS TURNED UPSIDE DOWN BY THE DEATH OF HIS ADORED FATHER, WHILE KATHARINE WORSLEY PASSED A SERENE CHILDHOOD IN A SMALL YORKSHIRE VILLAGE

THE DUKE OF KENT'S FIRST CHILD TOOK almost 48 hours to be born and his entry into the world was watched over by a strange guardian. While Prince George, the Royal Family and the world waited on tenterhooks, there was another curious attendant at the birth. Family legend has it that on the evening of 9 October 1935, when Marina had been in labour for many hours, a black cat took up station outside their Belgravia home until the baby was born five hours later in the early hours of 10 October.

To some a black cat symbolizes good luck, and to others bad. The infant Edward George Nicholas Paul Patrick would seem to have been the luckiest child in the world. Seventh in line of succession to the throne, born to adoring parents very much in love, his life seemed set fair. But as time progressed, this unknown feline was to cast a dark shadow of tragedy over the young Prince's life.

Sixth in line

But that lay in the future. Edward's early childhood was idyllic. He was christened in the Chapel Royal in St James's Palace, wearing the traditional Royal christening robe. The new baby was a hit with the whole family, especially his grandfather, who adored him. But George V's health was failing fast and the baby's first Christmas was destined to be the grandfather's last. It was spent at Sandringham, and the King was distressed when it was time for them to go. Before the end of January he was dead, and Edward was now sixth in line to the throne.

Edward's main Christmas present the following year was the birth of his sister, Princess Alexandra, on Christmas morning. But the baby was of no great interest to the toddler, who was already showing signs of being Daddy's boy. Edward trailed his father everywhere, and George was an excellent father. One of Marina's friends, Baroness Agnes de Stoeckel, was amused by this bond between father and son,

♛ *The Duke was a devoted father* above left *and remained at his wife's side throughout most of her labour with Edward* far right*, only to miss the actual birth when he went to snatch a few hours' sleep.* Below *Edward and his four-year-old sister Alexandra play on the beach at St Margaret's Bay, while their parents are abroad. The war years were to separate the family for weeks at a time*

which had begun when Edward was very young. 'Every evening, instead of sitting late as usual,' she reported, 'he leaves the table shortly after ten o'clock and carries his son to the nursery and lays him on his cot and stands watching and waiting. Nanny told me that each night as he lays his son in his cot... she can hear the Duke talking softly to him.'

As he grew older Edward saw his father as the fount of all knowledge. George taught him how to strip and reassemble a complex toy motor

Hulton Picture Company

'*He has fine blue eyes,*
golden curls and
looks like all four Georges
rolled into one'

A FAMILY FRIEND ON BABY EDWARD

interests were mechanical, and whose parents had allowed him to run free. She prized good behaviour, and she set about teaching her grand-children the essential royal quality of restraint and imbuing them with her own sense of awe and respect for royal history and tradition. She improved Edward's reading, and took both chil-dren on educational rides around the countryside, perched in a horse-drawn farm-cart to save petrol.

His father's visits were always a high point for Edward. Queen Mary strictly observed wartime rationing, so after bleak meals of dried egg it seemed doubly miraculous when George turned up with a crate each of bananas and oranges. These fruits, unknown during the war, were a gift from the President of the United States. To the little boy, it must have seemed that his father who 'knew everything' could do anything as well.

A new brother

In 1942 the family was completed by the birth of Michael. Edward was old enough to take more interest in this new baby, helped by the fact that his mother strongly believed it was her duty to 'prepare a young child for the advent of an infant brother or sister'.

The important thing was for the family to be together again. It was a hot summer and Edward and Alexandra left Badminton for a while to be with their parents and the new baby. But just over

♛ *Windsor Wings For Victory* left, *June 1943. An excited Edward and his mother find a moment of relief from their sorrow at one of the wartime events held to raise funds for buying aircraft*

car and was always patiently ready to answer the dozens of questions Edward put to him.

When not in Belgrave Square, the young family spent their time at Coppins, the family home in Buckinghamshire. For Edward and Alexandra these were idyllic times with their parents. But when war broke out Coppins seemed increasingly unsafe, situated as it was beneath the flight path of German bombers on route for London, and the two young children were sent to stay with their grandmother at Badminton House in Gloucestershire. Edward was six at the time, and this enforced separation from his parents must have seemed hard. Marina visited when she could, and his beloved father was also able to visit while carrying out his duties as Air Commodore in charge of welfare of the Air Force. But occasional visits did not compensate for the closeness that had gone before, and for a boy who had idolized his father, a grandmother, however doting, was no substitute.

But Queen Mary was to have a good and for-mative influence on the little boy whose main

a month later, Edward's life was turned upside down. His adored father was killed in a plane crash, and his previously light-hearted mother was prostrate with grief. Edward was six-and-a-half when this happened, too young to understand anything but that his father was gone forever and his mother lost in shock and grief. Now he was the Duke of Kent in his father's place.

Queen Mary rushed to the side of her daughter-in-law and took over much of the care of the three children. A woman who was used to dealing with grief herself – having buried her husband and another of her sons – she was able to give to Edward some of the stability he so desperately needed, despite the fact that it was her favourite son who had died.

Life was very different for Edward after this, even when his mother bravely rallied and began to rebuild her life. For Marina had little money of her own and the Royal purse had no automatic provision for his surviving widow.

An austere life

Marina managed by economizing and reluctantly accepting financial help from the family, but nevertheless the life of the Kent children was austere compared to what it had been. There was less automatic contact with the Royal Family and Edward learned the simple pleasures of the seaside in summer and quiet family togetherness the rest of the year.

The previously exuberant Edward had been clearly marked by his father's death. According to Princess Margaret's suitor, Group-Captain Peter Townsend, 'Prince Eddie...was diffident, hypersensitive.' This was a kindly way of saying that Edward was often withdrawn, but that

Ray Duns

3 BELGRAVE SQUARE

Edward's earliest memories were of his London home at 3 Belgrave Square. The small house, on the south side of the square, had a connection with the Kents: Queen Victoria's mother, also Duchess of Kent, had once lived there. It now belonged to a friend of Queen Mary's, who had let the couple have a free hand when she rented it to them. By the time Edward was old enough to notice his surroundings, his father had transformed the dark, heavy, over-stuffed rooms into an exquisite showcase of art treasures, set against the light pastels he preferred. Queen Mary, from whom George had inherited his taste for interior decoration, had supervised the first redecoration while George and Marina were on their honeymoon

Edward's little brother Michael was born on 4 July 1942 at Coppins. The christening photograph left *included (sitting, from left to right) Princess Elizabeth, Lady Patricia Ramsay, HM the Queen, Prince Edward, Queen Mary, Princess Alexandra, Marina with Michael, the Dowager Marchioness of Milford Haven, Crown Princess Marthe of Norway, Princess Margaret and Princess Helena Victoria. In the back row are Princess Marie Louise, Prince Bernhard of the Netherlands, King George VI, Prince George, King Haakon of Norway, King George of the Hellenes and Crown Prince Olaf of Norway.* Right *Summer at Coppins, 1945. After Prince George's death, Marina became father and mother to her young family*

Popperfoto

emotion would often burst forth into a temper tantrum. It is also significant that he began to suffer from asthma – an illness that can be connected to emotional stress – shortly after his father died. Alone with his mother, he would pour out his anguish about his father; he mentioned him constantly.

Marina felt that he needed a male influence in his life, and appointed a young history master at Eton, Giles St Aubyn, to tutor Edward part-time and to act as a friend to him. St Aubyn took Eddie on walking holidays, gently encouraging his interests and introducing him to new subjects.

> ## 'She was a delightful child to have in a class; very merry and bright and ready for a bit of mischief'
>
> HER FORM MISTRESS ON KATHARINE

Fortunately Marina's choice was good and, with the undivided attention he was given, Edward blossomed. His asthma attacks were reduced and he gradually learned to handle his powerful emotions in a less destructive way. Slowly he developed self-confidence, which stopped him withdrawing and, rather than be overwhelmed by his temper, he started to channel his aggression into more useful assertiveness.

Edward's education was now at issue. It had been his father's wish that Edward should go to Eton (George had wanted to put his name down when he was only four months old), and he arrived as a new boy in 1948. Education did not make a scholar of Edward. He did not distinguish himself, either at Eton or at Le Rosay in Switzerland, which he attended later. School only served to convince him that he wanted to make a career as a professional soldier, so Sandhurst seemed the logical next step.

Introducing Kate

In 1939 Edward's father, the Duke of Kent, had paid an official visit to Hovingham in North Yorkshire. He was a man who adored children, and he found himself drawn to an enchanting little six-year-old. Katharine was the daughter of Sir William Worsley, Lord Lieutenant of the North Riding of Yorkshire, President of the MCC and country squire. Kate was very keen to talk to the Royal visitor. The Duke picked up the little

Popperfoto

👑 *Dressed in the college's distinctive uniform of waistcoat, tails and striped trousers, a 14-year-old Edward escorts his mother and sister around the grounds at an Eton cricket match in 1950 above. A shy and sensitive teenager, he had already borne the title of Duke of Kent for more than half his young life*

girl and, with the same patience he used with his own son, answered all the questions she put to him.

The Worsleys had no royal connections or titles, but they came from a distinguished and wealthy family that could trace its ancestry back to the 11th century. The family had lived in Hovingham Hall – a large manor house set in 4000 acres – since 1723, and it was 210 years later that Katharine was born there, on 22 February 1933.

Katharine's brief brush with Royalty became a family anecdote, but certainly did not give the child ideas about attaining Royal status herself.

She was a good, hard-working, modest child, educated at home by a governess until the age of ten. Kate was something of a tomboy and loved country pursuits – although she did not like horses as much as dogs. She did not have the usual little girl's love of dressing up; the village postmistress said, 'The only thing she cared about was her hair. Even as a small child she always wanted it to look nice.'

When war came, Kate was only six-and-a-half. The village became home to 60 small evacuees as well as quite a few soldiers who camped in the grounds around Hovingham Hall, preventing the little girl from wandering or riding freely around, as she used to do. But Diana Colgate, a young cousin, came to stay at the Hall and provided a companion for Kate, whose brothers were away at school.

At 12, Katherine went as a day girl to St Margaret's School in Castle Howard, the home of the Howard family and then, after two years, to Runton Hill School in Norfolk as a boarder.

♛*Katharine, the youngest of the four Worsley children and the only girl, grew up in the small and friendly village of Hovingham right, 20 miles north-east of York. Pretty, friendly and kindhearted, she began helping her mother with village work at a young age and was much beloved by the local families*

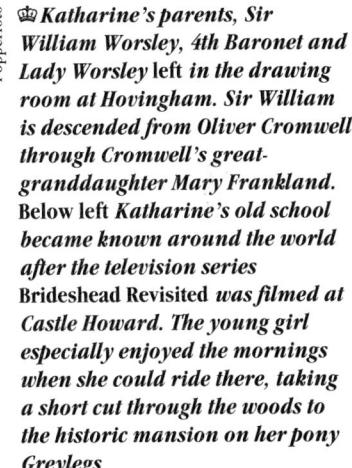

AA Photo Library

Popperfoto

♛*Katharine's parents, Sir William Worsley, 4th Baronet and Lady Worsley left in the drawing room at Hovingham. Sir William is descended from Oliver Cromwell through Cromwell's great-granddaughter Mary Frankland. Below left Katharine's old school became known around the world after the television series* Brideshead Revisited *was filmed at Castle Howard. The young girl especially enjoyed the mornings when she could ride there, taking a short cut through the woods to the historic mansion on her pony Greylegs*

Carol Kane

For a while she longed to finish her education at Oxford University, where her brothers Marcus, John and Oliver had studied but, though she was clever, she was not clever enough so, although Katharine did finish her education at Oxford, it was at Miss Hubler's, a young ladies' finishing school. Here the accent was on feminine accomplishments such as dressmaking and cookery, although academic subjects which could improve a young lady's conversation were encouraged: she studied French literature, history, painting and architecture. She also studied music, one of her great and continuing loves. She left at 18, an attractive but unstylish girl, driven by her love of music and a sense of mission. Finishing school traditionally prepares a girl for a good marriage, but Katharine wanted to work with children and was determined to put her energies into charity work.

Two years later, in 1953, her parents were invited to be guests at the Coronation of Queen Elizabeth II. This was in recognition of her father's distinguished position, not a sign of particular friendship. The Worsleys brushed shoulders with Royalty, but no closer connection was thought of at all.

HEIRLOOMS AND HONOURS

Though less ostentatious than other members of her family, when the occasion demands, Katharine can put on a glittering show. Most of her finest pieces of jewellery, including a number of priceless Romanov treasures, were gifts from Princess Marina. Her husband, as personal aide-de-camp to the Queen, makes many public appearances in the dress uniform of Colonel of the Scots Guards

♛The Duke of Kent has always been an indefatigable representative of the Royal Family on state occasions at home and abroad: *above* as a member of the House of Lords in state robes for the opening of Parliament, *below* attending the independence ceremonies for Sierra Leone in 1961, wearing the tropical dress uniform of his regiment. He has represented the Queen in a similar capacity in over 50 countries round the world, from the United States of America to the People's Republic of China

♛Arriving at a banquet for the President of Italy held at the Victoria and Albert Museum in October 1990 *right*, Katharine appears at her most formal in a pearl and diamond necklace and tiara. On her hip, she has incorporated the badge of the Royal Victorian Order into her outfit with stunning effect

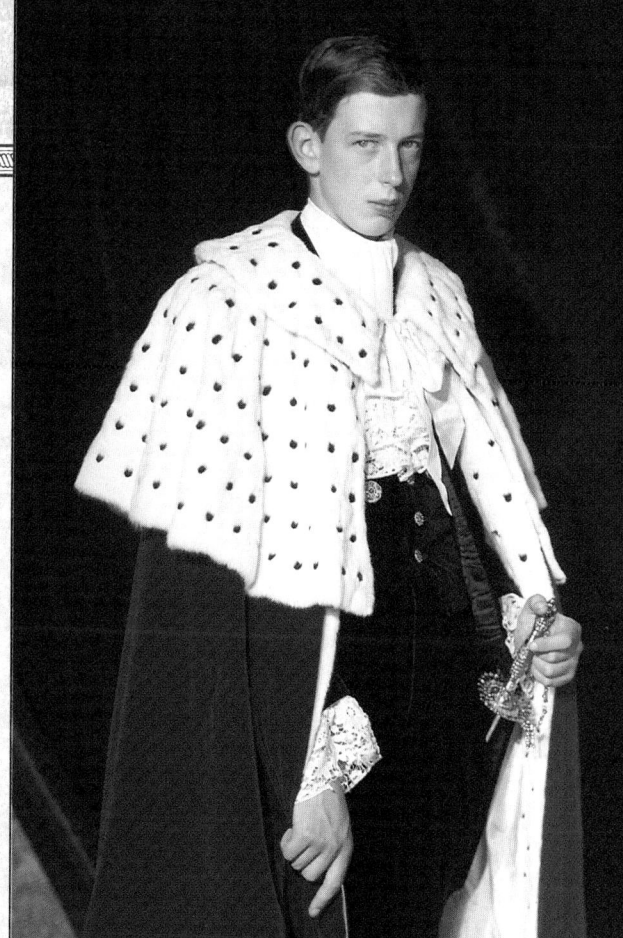

Cecil Beaton/Camera Press

Barry Lategan/Camera Press

Camera Press

☙A Duke and Duchess in all their finery, April 1972 *above*. Katharine has on the diamond tiara that she wore at her wedding: this was a present from Marina, as was her diamond and pearl bracelet. Edward is in the dress uniform of the Royal Scots Greys with the sash, badge and star of the Order of St Michael and St George and the star of the Royal Victorian Order

☙Seventeen-year-old Edward wore the ermine and velvet robes of a Royal Duke at Elizabeth II's Coronation *above right*. He and the other Royal Dukes placed coronets on their head at the same time as the Crown of St Edward was placed on the Queen's head. Thirteen years later, in 1966, Edward's wife Katharine was made Chancellor of Leeds University – the youngest in the history of that University. She is shown *right* in May 1968, wearing the robes of Chancellor as she presides over the conferment of degrees. One of her tasks was to bestow an honorary doctorate of law on her father

F ALLING IN LOVE

Popperfoto

EDWARD HAD NOT BEEN LONG IN YORKSHIRE BEFORE HE MET THE GIRL WHO WOULD MAKE HIS EXILE FROM LONDON A DELIGHT

S ANDHURST CONTINUED THE PROCESS THAT Giles St Aubyn and Eton had started. Training in leadership qualities and all the rigorous physical activity now gave Edward the outward appearance of a confident young man. But as yet there was no sign of maturity; rather the reverse. It was as if Edward was making up for the childhood he had lost to grief and early responsibility. Hesitancy and lack of assurance were now replaced by the *joie de vivre* that he had had before his father died.

👑 *The death of George VI in 1952, and the accession of the young Queen Elizabeth, meant that more royal duties needed to be shared out among the family: Edward accompanied his mother on an official tour of Malaya while he was still a schoolboy below. But later, as an Army officer above, he was not expected to attend as many official engagements as his mother or sister*

After leaving Sandhurst in 1955, Edward entered the Royal Scots Greys as a second lieutenant. Now a real professional soldier, he was nevertheless still a young man bent on having fun. His spare time in London was spent in nightclubs, or in speeding recklessly back and forth in his car. His feeling of invincibility was increased when he was able to walk away from one car which he had written off, but in another crash he was not so lucky, barely escaping with his life.

The following summer he was posted with his regiment to Catterick camp in the North Riding of Yorkshire. As far as Edward was concerned, this was yet more bad luck. Being buried in the wilds of Yorkshire seemed to him like a prison sentence.

> ## 'A vivacious girl,
> ## sparkling with her love of
> ## music and the theatre
> ## and her interest in
> ## people'
>
> A FRIEND ON KATHARINE

Edward's social life now became relentlessly sedate. The top social event was an invitation to lunch from his aunt, the Princess Royal, at Harewood House near Leeds. Alexandra alerted her old schoolfriends in the area to Edward's presence and they included him in their invitations, but the parties of carefully brought-up debs seemed tame after the seductive dangers of London's nightlife. In October, Edward turned 21. His mother gave a birthday party for him at Coppins, which bristled with Royalty, including

Camera Press

himself sitting next to on that autumn Sunday was very different from the girls he met at nightclubs. She was undeniably as beautiful: slender, blonde, with a long aristocratic neck. But unlike those other girls, she was quiet, modest and serious-minded. They talked diffident!y, as two people do who are searching for subjects in common, and they found they shared an enthusiasm for music and art. Later, Katharine showed Edward round Hovingham Hall, pointing out the collections of old masters and drawings. He stood for a while, admiring a portrait of Katharine by Sir Timothy Eden. 'Ah,' he commented, 'it doesn't do you justice, Miss Worsley.'

A guest at Hovingham Hall

Edward soon became a regular visitor. But it was not just the comfort and friendliness of the Worsley establishment that drew him. He wanted to know Katharine better, and very soon the formality of their first meeting evaporated. Katharine was more mature than Edward, perhaps overly serious. As he responded to the challenge of her refined nature, so she began to take delight in his more carefree boyishness. Edward brought over rock and roll records and taught her how to dance as they did in the clubs. She retaliated by teaching him the more classic steps of the waltz. Edward took her to dances and introduced her to the exhilaration of fast cars by trips to the race track at Silverstone. Within weeks they had fallen in love.

By Christmas it seemed intolerable to Edward that they would have to spend any time apart. He was expected to spend the festive

the Queen and Prince Philip. Three weeks later, Edward set off dutifully for yet another tedious social engagement.

This was a Sunday lunch party given by Sir William Worsley, who routinely invited the new officers at Catterick to join his family for lunch at Hovingham Hall. The seating plan arranged for Edward to sit next to Sir William's 23-year-old daughter, Katharine.

The young woman whom Edward found

♛ *Edward's love of fast cars led him into several scrapes. On 20 June 1954 his Hillman was involved in a collision* top, *and he was taken to hospital*

♛ Above *Katharine was quick to notice that her pet poodle, Charles, who normally disliked strangers, took to Edward and followed him around*

♛ *Edward – with companion and false moustache left – was a dedicated party-goer when he met Katharine, but she did not share his love of nightlife*

season at Sandringham, as tradition demanded. But he was determined to see Katharine if he could.

Marina knew something of Katharine, but was unprepared for Edward's announcement on Christmas Day that he was very much in love and wanted to seek permission to visit Katharine on Boxing Day. She advised him against asking the Queen for quite unprecedented leave, but perhaps Edward understood his cousin better than his mother did. At tea time he asked the Queen if she would release him the next day. The Queen, remembering what it was like to be young and in love, gave her permission immediately.

Marina's worries

Marina could not now be unaware of the strength of Edward's feelings and she was not happy about them. He had a record of impulsive behaviour: he had only recently recovered from his car crash and only weeks ago he had been plunged into despondency by his removal from

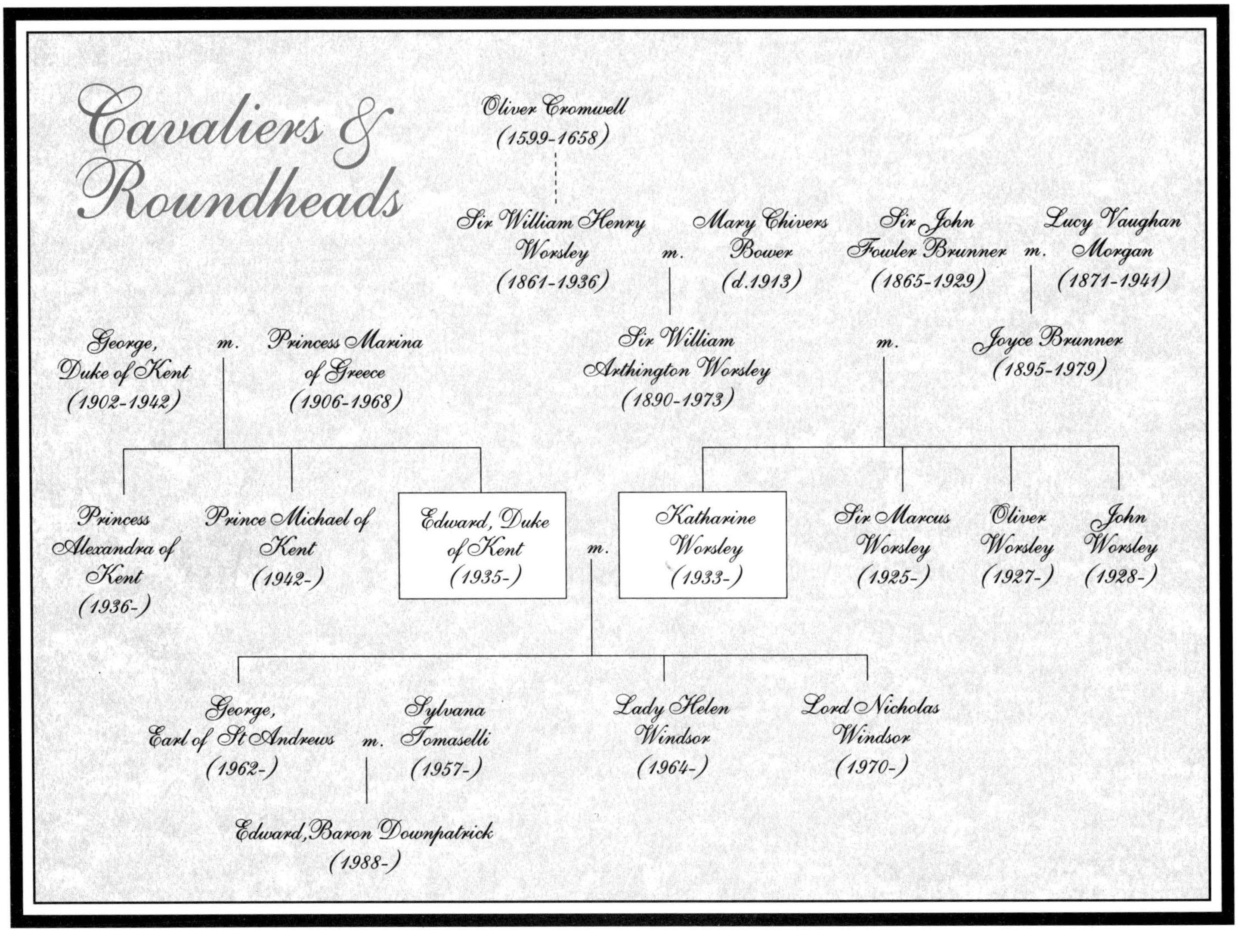

Cavaliers & Roundheads

Oliver Cromwell
(1599-1658)

Sir William Henry Worsley (1861-1936) m. Mary Chivers Bower (d.1913)

Sir John Fowler Brunner (1865-1929) m. Lucy Vaughan Morgan (1871-1941)

George, Duke of Kent (1902-1942) m. Princess Marina of Greece (1906-1968)

Sir William Arthington Worsley (1890-1973) m. Joyce Brunner (1895-1979)

Princess Alexandra of Kent (1936-)

Prince Michael of Kent (1942-)

Edward, Duke of Kent (1935-) m. Katharine Worsley (1933-)

Sir Marcus Worsley (1925-)

Oliver Worsley (1927-)

John Worsley (1928-)

George, Earl of St Andrews (1962-) m. Sylvana Tomaselli (1957-)

Lady Helen Windsor (1964-)

Lord Nicholas Windsor (1970-)

Edward, Baron Downpatrick (1988-)

Hulton Picture Company

SANDHURST

The Royal Military Academy at Sandhurst has had many Royal pupils in its time. Edward would have been expected to prove himself competent under the military training as well as in the academic subjects, such as mathematics, science, languages, physics and problems of government. Other activities – mountaineering, exploration and ocean sailing – are undertaken to develop leadership qualities. The course lasted 18 months at the time when Edward was there and he graduated 44th out of 220. The order of merit is determined by a combination of personal and leadership qualities and how well each candidate has done on the course. Each term the Queen's Medal Prize for best overall results in military and practical tests is awarded to the first cadet and the Sword of Honour to the cadet considered by the commandant to be the best of the term. Edward himself was awarded the Sir James Moncrieff Grierson Prize for Languages

the nightclubs of London. Now he seemed to be talking wildly of love and even marriage. She thought that it was another phase that would all too quickly pass. After all, he was barely 21 and young for his years. Katharine sounded a nice girl, but there were other beautiful girls around and Edward had plenty of time. She hoped that this passion, like others, would blow over, but meanwhile she was determined to act as a restraining influence.

By Easter it was clear that this particular passion was going to last longer than a few short weeks. Edward spent his Easter leave as a guest of Sir William's at Hovingham Hall. Until now, he had always spent all his leave with his mother and Marina felt it was time to take a more active interest in this youthful romance. She invited Katharine to spend Whitsun at Coppins.

Marina must have been surprised and pleased to make Katharine's acquaintance. Here was a young woman of real calibre and beauty and she seemed to be in love with Edward. But if Edward had hoped that his mother's good impression of Katharine would affect her feelings about a marriage he was sadly mistaken.

Too young to marry

It was undeniable that Edward was very young to be thinking of marriage. He was also a Royal Duke and his wife would become a Royal Duchess. To Marina, this meant that making the right match involved far more than love or even choosing a woman who was pleasant, well-educated and sound. She had in mind for Edward a bride who was born to the rigours of royal duty.

♛ *Shortly before she met Edward, Katharine had given up her job as a kindergarten teacher in London to help her mother who was suffering from arthritis. This allowed her to play a more active part in Yorkshire social life, but she also took over much of the charity work that her mother was now too ill to undertake* below

Edward now made it plain that he wanted to marry Katharine, and his mother made it equally plain that he would not have her blessing. As a Royal under the age of 25, he would also need the consent of the Queen to marry, and she would obviously be reluctant to grant it in the face of his mother's disapproval.

Edward's youth showed in his handling of his mother's steadfastness. He threatened to

Popperfoto

Hulton Picture Company

the more she had been able to understand how very different royal life was. The Queen Mother had undergone much the same experience when she was courted by the Duke of York, so she would have been able to understand the way Katharine was torn by her love for Edward and the reality of marrying into the Royal Family.

Meanwhile, Edward's campaign seemed to be paying off. A few weeks later, on 10 July, the Queen and Prince Philip called in on Katharine and her family at Hovingham Hall while on an official tour of Yorkshire. This was public recognition of the best kind.

In February 1958, Edward took Katharine to Clarence House to meet Princess Margaret and they too got on well. By now most of the family had met Katharine and no-one had a word to say against her. Indeed it was obvious that she was good for Edward and that their love had now stood the test for more than a year. But if Edward was feeling optimistic, his younger sister was more realistic. 'They'll advise delay,' Alexandra predicted gloomily, 'They always do.'

Katharine's doubts

Katharine herself was becoming even less sure as the months went by. She knew she loved Edward but she had begun to wonder if this was enough. She was somewhat shy and retiring, and seeing how Princess Alexandra – more than three years younger than herself – had to deal with the press

elope with Katharine anyway, if permission was refused. Indeed, he begged Katharine to take this course with him 'and hang the consequences'. But Katharine was understandably alarmed at the turn of events. She was very much in love with Edward, but the idea of marrying him against his family's wish gave her pause. She asked him to give her more time to think.

A new plan of action

After some reflection, Edward began a more considered campaign. He felt that the more members of his family who met and liked Katharine, the more likely he was to succeed in marrying her. In June 1957 he prevailed on his aunt, the Queen Mother, to invite Katharine to lunch at the Royal Lodge. The Queen Mother immediately took to Katharine, perhaps seeing something of herself in the young girl. The closer Katharine had drawn to Edward's family,

♛ *Katharine was keen to share her love of music with Edward, and he wanted to introduce her to the excitement of motor racing by taking her to Silverstone above. But their days of carefree enjoyment were soon to end, and the terrible prospect of a year's separation hung over them*

♛ *While Edward was stationed at Catterick, he escorted the Queen during her inspection of his own regiment, the Royal Scots Greys, of which she was Colonel in Chief right. The Queen was well aware of the obstacles being placed in the path of Edward and Katharine's romance, but she shared Marina's opinion that it would be better for them to wait a while before they committed themselves to marriage*

PA/Topham

Gala Diner

Popperfoto

FAMOUS FRIENDS

Edward's formative years were enlivened by many of his parents' famous friends. After his father died, many of them continued to visit Marina and her children regularly. Malcolm Sargent, the conductor; actor Douglas Fairbanks; photographer Cecil Beaton and the writer Somerset Maugham were four of the most frequent guests. Danny Kaye, the American actor and comedian, used to make Marina's family his first port of call whenever he was in London, and his visits were most popular with Edward, as Kaye left him helpless with laughter. Noël Coward remained a close friend of Marina's throughout her life. Her butler remembers an occasion when Coward was singing and playing the piano for guests at Kensington Palace. Edward's dog sidled up to the instrument and cocked his leg against it. 'You see,' said Coward drily, 'Not only an actor but a critic too'

and the public seemed daunting.

Even the prospect of the wedding unnerved Katharine. The idea of a lavish state occasion in Westminster Abbey was more than she could bear. Never mind, her suitor was anxious to assure her, they could be married in the small church at Hovingham if she preferred. Carried away by enthusiasm, Edward even proposed this idea to his horrified mother. It could not have been more ill-timed. This crystallized Marina's objections: it proved to her that her son was too young to understand his obligations as a Royal

'I have never seen a couple so enchanted with one another'

A FRIEND

Duke and it further put in doubt Katharine's suitability as a Royal consort.

Perhaps, with Katharine's help, Edward could have pursued his plan of gradually bringing the family round to his way of thinking. But in August 1958, he heard that he was to be posted to Germany for two years. It now became imperative that the proposed marriage should receive both the maternal and the Royal blessing.

But, incredibly, Marina stood firm. Indeed, she said she would only reconsider if Edward agreed not to see Katharine for an entire year. In this, she said, she had the Queen, Prince Philip and the Queen Mother on her side. Marina had

convinced them that it was too soon to know whether Edward knew his own mind. The Royal Family had spoken: Edward had to wait. Katharine knew her own family would follow the Royal line. There was nothing to be done.

In 1958 Lord Astor invited Katharine to holiday aboard his yacht below. It may have been a good omen, as Edward's parents had also cruised with the Astors

AP/Topham

♛This simple dress with its clean, uncluttered lines *left* was a style much favoured by the Duchess. The French designer Courrèges revolutionized the shape of dresses by dismissing the dart, and the length by finishing daringly above the knee. Katharine, with her enthusiasm for this new, unstuffy style of *haute couture*, patronized some of the top fashion houses. Her silvery blonde hair sets off the bold, bright colours

♛Katharine's striking outfits were much photographed and, from head to toe, her good dress sense shows. Eye-catching hats soon became one of the Duchess's hallmarks. This jaunty hat, matching the equally bold coat *below*, shows the importance of hats in the royal image. The strong lines of the hat and coat are echoed by the bold buckles on matching patent belt and shoes

This neat dress is given its shape entirely by using seaming. The style of this dress is a typical sixties design

Dress trimmed at the neckline, sleeves and hem with a contrasting colour self-fabric.

Outfit completed with duo-tone court shoes, which pick up the white trim of the dress

Lynne Robinson

PA/Topham

SUNNY ELEGANCE

In the swinging 'sixties, Katharine was the first member of the Royal Family to be photographed wearing a miniskirt. Her passion for up-to-the-minute fashion has always been balanced by the elegant and romantic creations she wears for state occasions, and she would now be likely to smile at some of her earlier outfits

A feature of Katharine's millinery wardrobe is to match the hat to the outfit, often with the same fabric. This strong 'seventies design *below left*, complete with elegant tassel, is a perfect example. Another coat and hat ensemble in the same fabric *below*: the baubles on this 'sixties creation are cheeky yet sophisticated, with a contrasting trimming

Hulton Picture Company

Topham

PA/Topham

Jim Bennett/Alpha

Voted one of the best-dressed women in the world on several occasions, Katharine is impeccably groomed even for informal events. Here *far left*, she looks every bit the smart traveller after stepping off a plane. An understated veiled hat completes a 'sixties wool suit with silk detail to match the blouse worn underneath. *Left* The same idea is used in a more recent outfit. A linen jacket and silk print dress are complemented by a matching hat

Cossack-style hat trimmed to match outfit

The 'sixties and 'seventies were times of fun, trendsetting fashions. The 'eighties brought more flexible styles with fewer fashion 'rules'. Skirts, for instance, could be on or way above the knee. With her elegant looks, these quieter, more sophisticated styles suited Katharine. Her choice of colours was still bold, and hats, as ever, dashing. The cossack style *left*, also a favourite with the Princess of Wales and the Duchess of York, looks particularly graceful, with an elongated peplum making a three-quarter length coat. Katharine's attention to detail is evident in the coat's smart black trimming and front fastening, and its co-ordinated hat

This stunning picture *right* was taken by the Royal photographer Norman Parkinson. Katharine's filmy, frothy dress was created by the Emanuel design team, to whom the Princess of Wales later went for her wedding-dress. With her luminous white dress and the blooms in her lap, the Duchess looks the true white rose of York

Three-quarter length coat is decorated with ornamental frog fastenings in black braid, at the centre front and cuffs

For premières and similar occasions, the Duchess looks simply elegant. Her choice of a striking jewel-blue evening-dress worn off the shoulder *below* highlights her matching set of diamond choker and earrings

This suit has been trimmed throughout with a contrasting black braid

Outfit is completed with black gloves, handbag and court shoes

LONG-AWAITED WEDDING

EDWARD AND KATHARINE SURVIVED THEIR LONG SEPARATION, AND EVEN FOUND THAT THEIR LOVE FOR EACH OTHER HAD GROWN. AT LONG LAST, THEY WERE ALLOWED TO WED

👑**Left** *Two years before her marriage, Katharine stands self-consciously beside the Duke of Atholl at a race meeting of the Perth Hunt*

👑**Below** *Princess Margaret and Antony Armstrong-Jones read some of telegrams congratulating them on their engagement. But their wedding was to mean further delay for Edward and Katharine*

Hulton Picture Company

EDWARD'S 23RD BIRTHDAY WAS A SAD AFFAIR. He spent it with Katharine and her parents at Hovingham Hall, all too aware that within five days he was to leave for his two-year stint in Germany.

By now Katharine had been able to convince Edward that there was no use in continuing to defy the family. A less impetuous person than Edward, she was able to look at matters in the long term. She felt as sure as she could be that their love would pass the test of a year apart, and she knew that showing that they could survive separation was the best way of convincing both families that their decision was considered and wise.

A stern test

But although Katharine could be sensible, she was as miserable as Edward. There must have been a small niggle of doubt about whether the test of time would work in their favour or not. They were very much in love at the moment, when they could have all the time they wanted together, but how would their feelings change when this was no longer possible? Certainly, she knew that Edward's mother expected him to feel differently when there was time and distance between them, and who was to say which woman knew him better? How would Edward cope, a young, eligible officer in a foreign land, with the added advantage of being Royal? Katharine knew that while she might baulk at the idea of Royal status, there were plenty of young women who would jump at the opportunity. Was it too much to expect a man of 23 to remain faithful during this time?

In some ways it is harder to be left than to leave, and Katharine's life at Hovingham seemed empty now Edward was gone. She began her usual preparations for the music festival, but her heart wasn't in it. It seemed sensible, therefore,

Hulton Picture Company

someone else on her travels – someone not constrained by his family from marrying her, who could offer her an existence not so limiting or daunting as life as a working Royal. He knew all too well that she was a beautiful young woman and that other men were likely to be after her.

But in the event neither of them needed to worry. The foundations of their love were strong enough to endure such a separation. Katharine saw the sights across the Atlantic, but she did not look at another man. Edward, the erstwhile clubber, forsook the kind of social life that brought

⚜ Preparing to board their train for Germany, the troops of the Royal Scots Greys were too busy with their kitbags to notice a passing Duke left. During his tour of duty in Germany Edward was able to escape to the ski-slopes of Kitzbühel in Austria below

Hulton Picture Company

to take up her brother John's invitation to stay with him and his wife Carolyn in Toronto.

Katharine went for a month and enjoyed herself there. She particularly welcomed the distracting company of her young niece Willa, and she determined to make a longer visit. The following year she was back, and this time she found herself a job working for an exclusive jewellers called Henry Birks and Sons. But she was frequently depressed, and did little but spend her time shuttling between work and home. 'It

'She was like a lost soul.

It was clear her heart was

3000 miles away'

A FRIEND ON KATHARINE

was obviously the most unhappy time of her life,' said a friend. 'She was like a lost soul. It was clear her heart was 3000 miles away.'

Life in Canada was apparently not distracting enough. To help dispel Katharine's mood it was suggested that she should leave John and the family to travel the United States by Greyhound Bus, a 10,000-mile round trip during which she visited the West Coast, the Grand Canyon and Mexico City, ending up in Washington DC.

Edward wanted Katharine to be happy, but part of him worried that she might meet

Popperfoto

♔ *After all the months of waiting and secrecy, the news of Edward and Katharine's engagement was finally made public on 9 March 1961, above. The proud Duke posed for the photographers with his bride-to-be in the garden of Kensington Palace right*

♔Above *Katharine clearly enjoyed the traditional ritual of showing off her engagement ring to her future sister-in-law, Princess Alexandra*

him into contact with other women and concentrated on race meetings. Inquisitive press cameras only ever caught him with his sister on his arm when he came back to England on leave.

When Katharine returned home there were still some months of the enforced separation left. She tried not to talk about Edward and her friends assumed that the relationship was over. Indeed, only a few close friends ever knew how strongly they felt about each other. Back in 1957 her father had said publicly, 'The Duke and my daughter are just good friends. A romance? Good gracious, I don't think so.'

Resistance starts to crumble

But for Katharine the period of waiting had been very instructive. The prospect of becoming a high-profile public figure was less disturbing than the idea of never being allowed to marry Edward at all. It was said that by the summer of 1959, when it was clear that the two young people were still very much in love, senior Royals were already relenting. The Queen and the Queen Mother felt they should be allowed to

see each other before the year was up. The Queen remembered her own parents' attempts to interest her in other young men besides Philip because they were considered too young.

Marina, however, felt differently. A contract was a contract, and all concerned had agreed to the year. Perhaps Marina had secretly hoped that the couple would decide to stay parted, and that she could swing into the role she had hoped to play for all her children: that of matchmaker offering suitably chosen partners. As it happens, it was a role that all three denied her.

In November 1959 the waiting period was up. Edward had been promoted to the rank of temporary captain and was now posted to the War Office in London. In an exchange of letters, it was agreed that his long-awaited reunion with Katharine would take place at his mother's apartment in Kensington Palace.

Too keen to embrace

Edward was waiting at the top of the stairs when Katharine was ushered into the hall. The romantic encounter was somewhat spoiled when, in his rush to greet her, Edward tripped and fell, and broke a bone in his foot. Within minutes, however, it was apparent that their feelings had remained the same – indeed had intensified – after the long months apart.

The couple could have been forgiven for expecting that their patience was to be rewarded by an immediate engagement with a date set for the wedding. But yet again they were to be disappointed by the intrusion of royal protocol.

For Princess Margaret, too, was in love. She had received a proposal from Antony Armstrong-Jones, the society photographer, and the Queen had given her blessing to the match. Princess Margaret's marriage had, of course, to take priority, and it was unthinkable to have two Royal

Popperfoto

THE WEDDING-DRESS

Katharine's gown was made of shimmering white raw silk, with patterned gauze set within layers of organdie. It was beautifully simple, with a round neck emphasized by a plain row of pearls. The bride confessed, 'My mother-in-law chose that for me. She had an extraordinary taste in dress and I was very happy to be dressed by her. I had very little idea about what I liked in the way of clothes and I was very happy for her to train me.' The 15-foot train of pleated gauze fell from a tiara, a loan from Marina. At one point the train caught on a pew and it looked as if crown and veil would be pulled away, but quick thinking saved the day

Hulton Picture Company

♛ *The young couple shared one of the more carefree moments in the months leading up to their wedding during a day out at the Goodwood spring meeting* left

weddings separated by less than a year.

There was nothing to be done. The announcement of Margaret's engagement was made in February 1960 and her marriage took place in Westminster Abbey on 6 May. Edward and Katharine would have to wait even longer.

But this waiting period was different. It was now acknowledged that it was just a question of time for Edward and Katharine. Marina could be as charming as she could be obdurate. Now that she knew that Katharine was to be her daughter-in-law, she took the young woman under her own wing, and with the help of Alexandra the Royal apprenticeship began. Katharine was tutored in the thousand and one matters that a Royal lady must know as a matter of course. In a way Katharine was lucky that there was a further

YORK MINSTER

York Minster (the Cathedral of St Peter) was built on the site of a church founded by Edwin, King of Northumbria, in AD 627. It is England's largest medieval cathedral. Portions of the building date back to the reconstruction that began in 1070. It is especially famous for its stained glass, much of it medieval. During World War 1 most of the glass was removed and hidden. After this all the 109 stained glass windows were renovated, including the great 13th-century grisaille glass of the 'Five Sisters' window in the north transept. The cost was borne by the women of Britain as a memorial to the women of the Empire who died during the Great War. The marriage of Edward and Katharine was the first Royal wedding to be celebrated in the Minster since Edward II married Philippa of Hainault in 1328

period of time to wait. Princess Michael has always bemoaned the fact that Marina had died before she married Prince Michael, and therefore she had no-one to teach her royal ways. In recent times, the Princess of Wales and the Duchess of York have had to do all their learning in public, as their romances became common knowledge within weeks of starting.

So 1961 was to be Edward and Katharine's year. Their engagement was announced on 8 March 1961, nearly six years after their first meeting. That same week Katharine attended a state dinner for the Commonwealth Prime Ministers at Buckingham Palace. Observers judged her to be relaxed and confident. The training from Marina and Alexandra had paid off beautifully.

Their turn at last

The arrangements for the wedding now had to be made. It turned out to be lucky that their wedding had been preceded by Margaret's. Now there was less pressure to make it a grand state occasion, following on, as it did, so soon after Margaret's splendid ceremony. Of course, the small church at Hovingham was out of the question, but when Katharine quietly but firmly expressed a preference to be married at York

♛ *The spectacular nave of York Minster* left *was a scene to rival any of the more traditional venues for Royal weddings. Those who arrived early to wait outside the Minster* inset *sat through the morning drizzle with commendable British patience*

♛ *The Duke was able to relax a little, smiling to a friend as he passed through the guard of honour outside the Minster* above. *By the time the wedding party returned to Hovingham, the weather had brightened up, and the bride greeted local well-wishers with genuine enthusiasm as her train was manoeuvred through the gates of the hall* below

Minster rather than at Westminster Abbey, the Queen gladly granted her wish.

The wedding took place in York Minster on 8 June 1961, a morning which began with showers but soon turned into a perfect, sunny day. It was a formal wedding, but not overwhelmingly so – it was probably in the place and in the style that Katharine would have been married even if she had not chosen a Royal groom: her father's distinguished position would have ensured that some degree of grandeur was inevitable.

In the Minster Edward stood waiting for his bride, wearing the red tunic and full ceremonial dress of the Royal Scots Greys with the blue riband of the Grand Cross of the Victorian Order across his chest. Dotted around the Minster were soldiers from the Queen's Body Guard of the

Popperfoto

'She is absolutely right

'She is absolutely right for Eddie. A very nice girl and very English'

MARINA

ward as I was told. It was an extraordinary day.'

Together Marina and Katharine had chosen the Toccata in F from Widor's Fifth Symphony as the wedding march. The music so moved one of the bridesmaids, Princess Anne, that she later used it at her own wedding. A prayer, especially chosen by Katharine, summed up much of her own personality and attitude to life. Said to be composed by St Francis of Assisi, it included the words: 'Master, make us seek not so much to be consoled as to console, to be understood as to understand, to be loved as to love. For it is in giving that we receive; in self-forgetfulness that we find self; in pardon that we are pardoned ...'

Marina found this prayer so moving that it is said that she later learned it by heart. But this was not the only part of the service that moved her:

PA/Topham

Honourable Corps of Gentlemen-at-Arms, wearing fine red tunics and gold helmets with plumes. Edward's best man was his brother, Michael, wearing the dress uniform of a Sandhurst officer cadet. Prince Philip was uniformed too, wearing the distinctive scarlet and black of a Field Marshal.

All the Royal Family were present. The Queen wore a lilac outfit; her mother her favourite shade of pale turquoise. Princess Margaret was dressed in pale ice blue. Marina wore a magnificent dress of champagne-coloured silk embroidered with gold and silver, and carried a co-ordinating clutch bag. The Minster was filled with friends and family from the bride's side as well.

As the sun broke through, a fanfare of trumpets announced the arrival of the bride and her father. Katharine's memories are vague. 'It was all a dream, I couldn't believe what was happening,' she recalled years later. 'The church that I knew so well, where I'd played the organ, was suddenly transformed with television lights. I just did what I was told that day...just moved for-

♔*Katharine, in her blue silk going-away outfit, gave a respectful kiss to the head of her new family above. The newly-weds then boarded a Heron of the Queen's flight right, which flew them to Scotland for the first stage of their honeymoon*

as Edward made his vows to Katharine, she was seen to take a handkerchief from her bag and wipe the tears from her eyes.

When the ceremony was over the couple were driven to the reception in the Rolls-Royce with a transparent hood which the Queen had lent them for the occasion.

Break with tradition

Katharine was determined that the reception should be a family affair at Hovingham Hall, and she stipulated that she did not want any speeches. Neither were the wedding presents on display, as is usually the case at Royal weddings. In this way the couple were able to make a modest stand against royal tradition, and to reclaim the day as their own.

The wedding breakfast was served in marquees set up on the sloping lawns of Hovingham. The buffet meal comprised caviar, chicken, and strawberries and cream, followed by a splendid cake. Champagne flowed throughout the day, and the guests, spared the formality of a sit-down meal, were able to mingle freely, chat and laugh. Edward and Katharine had waited so long for this day that the last thing they were concerned with was eating. They slipped away when the party was still in full swing.

The first leg of the honeymoon was spent at Birkhall on the Balmoral estate in Scotland. On their arrival they found that the Queen had arranged for a hamper to await them, filled with

♛ *For the second, more exciting, part of the honeymoon, the Duke and Duchess flew from Scotland to Majorca, where they had been lent a villa belonging to Rolls-Royce millionaire Sir Whitney Straight* top. *Journalists and photographers did their best to spy on the honeymooners, but apart from a few innocent shots like this one of the couple driving their speedboat* above*, the Kents were allowed to taste the joys of married life in private*

champagne, coffee and sandwiches. After unwinding and recovering from the excitement of the day, they were ready to prepare themselves for the most romantic part of their honeymoon, to be spent in a Majorcan villa.

This was the start of married life together – a happiness that they had earned with patience and, finally, good grace. Neither of them have said that ultimately they regretted being made to wait. Edward was now undeniably more mature, and Katharine had been given the time she needed to prepare herself for her Royal role. Everyone now wished them well and, indeed, felt that they had proved that they had what it took to create a good and enduring marriage.

Marina was now able, with perfect sincerity, to say of Katharine, 'She is absolutely right for Eddie. A very nice girl and very English.'

Both Popperfoto

ROYAL RESIDENCE

ST JAMES'S PALACE

The Queen gave the Kent family a grace-and-favour London residence – York House in St James's Palace – soon after they sold Coppins, their family home in Buckinghamshire. The building of St James's Palace was begun in 1532, during the reign of Henry VIII, and some Tudor parts still survive. York House, the west wing of the Palace, has strong family memories: Edward's father, Prince George, lived there with the Duke of Windsor when both were young bachelors

♔The Guard Room *below*, with its magnificent decorative display of rifles and swords set against sombre green walls, still has its original Tudor fireplace. It stands as a reminder that during the Restoration the Palace was used as a state prison and a barracks

By Gracious Permission of HM the Queen

♔ *Left* The four-storey gatehouse with octagonal turrets is the main relic of Henry VIII's Palace, and it still has its original linenfold-panelled doors.

♔Guards march through Friary Court, one of the early Tudor courtyards *right*. Most of its buildings were destroyed by fire in 1809 and later rebuilt

♔St James's Palace was once the centre of Court ceremonial, and its State Rooms are particularly grand. The magnificent Banqueting Room *far right* was added during the reign of Queen Anne. Its decoration dates from 1821-23, and the red damask walls are hung with paintings of battles and state events

By Gracious Permission of HM the Queen

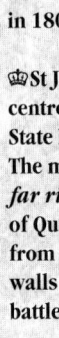

Spectrum

Although mostly redecorated in the 1830s, the Chapel Royal *right* retains its oak-coffered ceiling, painted in 1540 and attributed to Holbein. The Chapel has witnessed many Royal marriages, including Queen Victoria's and George V's. More recently, it saw the christening of Edward and Katharine's first grandchild

By Gracious Permission of HM the Queen

By Gracious Permission of HM the Queen

HOME AND ABROAD

AS AN OFFICER'S WIFE, KATHARINE FOLLOWED HER HUSBAND
AROUND THE WORLD. BUT EDWARD'S ROYAL POSITION AND
RESPONSIBILITIES EVENTUALLY FORCED HIM TO LEAVE THE ARMY,
AND THE YOUNG FAMILY SETTLED DOWN IN ENGLAND

ALTHOUGH EDWARD HAD LITTLE MONEY TO call his own, he did have a home to offer his new wife. Coppins had been left to him in his father's will, and Marina judged that it was now time she moved out and let the couple have it to themselves.

By now, Katharine's relationship with Marina was excellent, and she added her pleas to Edward's that her mother-in-law should continue to consider the house her own and stay as often as she liked. But Marina, now the Dowager Duchess of Kent, rightly considered this to be unsatisfactory for a newly married couple, and she made Kensington Palace her base exclusively: it was 'the only sensible thing to do'.

Not that they had much money with which to do this. Edward had his army pay, supplemented by interest from a few investments, made with

Left Edward and Katharine soon after their marriage. The new Duchess of Kent attracted a great deal of attention, but the couple's frequent absences abroad kept press coverage to a minimum

the small sum of money his father had left him in trust. As yet he was receiving no money from the Civil List, and Katharine, although she would one day inherit some money from her father, had no private income of her own.

First-born child

But money was not an issue with the Duke and his new Duchess. More would have been welcome, but they had never been under any illusions that they would be rich. They had, meanwhile, more important and distracting considerations. Soon after they were married Katharine discovered that she was pregnant, and on 26 June 1962 she gave birth to their first child, a son, whom they called George after his grandfather. The new baby also took the title of the Earl of St Andrews.

Edward, like his father, had planned to be present at the birth, but when his wife went into labour he set off for work at the War Office as usual, convinced that there would be a long wait. He had in mind the fact that, according to

Above The first photograph of George, Earl of St Andrews, taken on 16 July 1962. Mother and son were at Coppins, where the baby had been born just three weeks previously. George was tenth in line to the throne but not a prince – within the British Royal Family only the children and grandchildren of sovereigns can hold that title

Hulton Picture Company

While in Hong Kong in 1963, Edward below got a very public ducking when competing in a race at the Chinese Dragon Boat Festival. The Duke's boat, manned by soldiers from the 48th Gurkha Infantry Brigade, capsized halfway along the 900-yard course. Edward and the other crew-members had to push the boat home, dog-paddling as they went

AP/Topham

'We are delighted with my first granddaughter, especially as Katharine longed for a girl'

MARINA ON THE BIRTH OF HELEN

👑 *Helen and George* left *enjoy an outing with their parents to the Iver Village Fête, on a hot September day in 1966. They are applauding as the winners of a local beauty contest are announced. The village of Iver, in Buckinghamshire, is very close to Coppins, which was the Kent family home until the mid 1970s*

👑 *King Faisal of Saudi Arabia* below *chats with a smiling Duchess of Kent at a banquet given in the King's honour by the Lord Mayor of London in 1967. The shy Katharine Worsley has transformed herself into a Royal Duchess who can tackle the most formal occasions with aplomb*

family lore, his own birth took nearly two days, and that first children usually take longer to be born. In the event, his heir emerged quickly and without too much trouble while he was still at work, and the first he knew about it was from an excited phone call telling him that he now had a son. 'Good heavens,' was his immediate reaction, 'I thought they always arrived at dawn!'

It was about this time that Edward followed in his father's footsteps and became a Freemason. He planned to involve himself seriously in the activities of this secret society, but within months, in November 1962, he was posted to Hong Kong as second in command of C Squadron of the Royal Scots Greys.

Shortly before this, the Kents were invited to represent the Queen at the Ugandan Independence celebrations, and they took their new baby with them. This unprecedented move,

32

the first time such a young baby had accompanied its royal parents abroad, passed unnoticed – unlike the time the Princess of Wales, two decades later, chose to take her baby with her on a Royal tour. After all, Edward was a serving officer, and George, like other soldiers' babies, was destined for a childhood of travel.

The young family spent from November 1962 to November 1963 in Hong Kong. They were sad to leave Coppins, but in many ways the move suited them. Abroad it counted for little that they were members of the Royal Family. They could live their lives as ordinary people with no concession to their Royal status. For other couples this might have seemed a drawback, but uninterrupted time together out of the limelight was exactly what they wanted – and indeed was what they had dreamed of during their six years of courtship.

Being treated as an ordinary serving officer

👑*Right Edward in training for the European Two-Seater Bobsled Championship at Garmisch-Partenkirchen in Germany. Edward is a keen sportsman – he is particularly fond of skiing – and also interested in anything mechanical. He has held a pilot's licence for many years now*

👑*Edward and Katharine below talk together as they make their way to the paddock during the third day of the 1967 Royal Ascot race meeting. Royal Ascot is part of the English Season and every year the Royals – even those not known for a passionate interest in horse sports – turn out in force*

Topham

AP/Topham

did have some negative aspects. They swapped the elegance of Coppins for officer's quarters – a shabby second-floor three-bedroom flat with standard-issue furniture. Edward was working, and Katharine was able to devote herself to the baby. To help her look after George she had not only the expertise of the Scottish Miss Mary McPherson, but also a Chinese *ayah*. Katharine got on well with the other officer's wives, who had perhaps been initially wary of having a Royal Duchess in their midst. They found her refreshingly normal, and without 'side'.

No sooner had they returned from Hong Kong than they were off again. This time the posting was to Germany, where they were to spend the next two years. It was a much happier Duke of Kent who boarded the plane for Hanover than the man he had been in 1958 when a posting to Germany meant separation from Katharine. This time he took Katharine and his son with him.

Class of '64

But they were not destined to spend all of their time together. Within the year Katharine was pregnant again, and although parting from Edward was hard, she felt that she wanted to have her baby in England. In the spring of 1964 she flew back to England with her toddler son, to await the birth of the new baby.

Lady Helen Marina Lucy Windsor was born at Coppins on 29 April. Unusually for a Royal baby, Helen's birth attracted little attention – but that was not really surprising, for 1964 was Royal baby boom year. Baby Helen was preceded in February by her cousin, James Ogilvy (son of Princess Alexandra) and in March by Prince Edward, the Queen's last child. Following her in May came Lady Sarah Armstrong-Jones, the second child of Princess Margaret.

Edward left *leaves St Paul's Cathedral after being installed as Grand Master of the Order of St Michael and St George, one of the six orders of knighthood, in July 1968. More controversially, Edward is also Grand Master of the United Grand Freemasons' Lodge of England. He succeeded Lord Scarborough, who was Lord Chamberlain to the Queen, in 1966. George VI was also a Mason and Prince Philip became one to please his father-in-law. However, he has not been an active member, agreeing with his uncle Lord Louis Mountbatten that Freemasonry no longer serves any useful purpose. Both of them put pressure on Edward not to join, but his beloved father had been a Mason and he was determined to follow his example*

Right The Kents attend a memorial service for Princess Marina, held at Westminster Abbey on 25 October 1968. Princess Marina's untimely death from an inoperable brain tumour two months earlier, on 27 August, came as a sad shock to the Royal Family. She was only 61 years old. Although her illness had been diagnosed, she had been expected to live for some time longer. She was buried by her husband's side at Frogmore in Windsor Great Park

Hulton Picture Company

Popperfoto

By autumn 1965 the family was back in England and had taken up residence at Coppins again. Katharine devoted herself to her children and to creating a warm family atmosphere for her husband to return to when his duties were over. It had been a long time since the house had had young children in it, and it was as if it had been waiting for them. Investigation in the attic turned up some of Edward's old toys, which were dusted off and put into use again by his children. The swing in the garden built by Edward's father was now given a new lease of life by his grandchildren.

But this was the only way in which the house echoed the lifestyle of the previous Duke and Duchess of Kent. Marina and George had been social animals. They had filled Coppins with famous and talented guests. Katharine and Edward's favourite way of passing an evening

Alpha

ANMER HALL

Anmer Hall is some four miles from the Queen's house at Sandringham. Although fronted by a late-Georgian façade, much of the hall was actually built in the 17th century and a 'priest's hole' has been uncovered, where a priest could hide from the authorities in the days when England was a very dangerous place for a Catholic priest to be. Anmer has been linked to the Sandringham estate since before the Domesday Book was compiled in 1086. In those ancient days the manor of Sandringham was known as Sant-Dersingham. The then Prince of Wales (who was to become Edward VII) acquired Sandringham soon after his marriage in 1863 and in 1865 he bought land at Anmer as well. He liked to use it for shooting, as did his son, George V, who wrote in 1914 of 'more pheasants than I have ever seen there, we got 2,831'!

was *à deux*. Weekends were for spending time with their children, rather than at houseparties. When they did entertain, only family and close friends were invited.

Little George had a taste of life in the pubic eye for the first time when he was three-and-a-half, and he did not seem too thrilled about it. In January 1966 he was a pageboy at the wedding of Fiona Bowes-Lyon, a great niece of the Queen Mother, to Mr Joseph Goodheart. It was all too much for him, and he burst into tears in the middle of the ceremony.

George on stage

Much more to his taste was his Christmas treat later that same year. Katharine took George with a group of his friends to Sooty's Christmas Show in London. At one point, Harry Corbett (Sooty's puppeteer) invited young volunteers up on the stage to sing a song. Katharine watched, amused and proud, as her little son raced to be first. With some of his mother's musical talent and none of her shyness, George won first prize with his version of 'Away in a Manger'. The prize was a Sooty glove puppet, and when Harry Corbett presented it to George he asked him what his father did for a living. George thought hard before replying, 'He changes in and out of uniform.'

Towards the end of 1969, after a gap of over five years, the couple discovered, to their delight, that Katherine was pregnant again. On 25 July 1970 she gave birth to another son, Lord Nicholas Windsor. Since Katharine was now in her late thirties, Nicholas was born in King's College Hospital, London – the best place to be should the birth be complicated. His elder brother and sister had been born at home.

Tom Hustler/Camera Press

⚜**Above** *The family relax in the grounds at Coppins in 1969. George and Helen were happy, healthy and unspoilt. Their parents were careful to bring them up as simply and as far from the limelight as possible. Katharine gave birth to a second son the following year* below*: Nicholas Charles Edward Jonathan was born on 25 July*

Hulton Picture Company

A FAMILY OF FIVE

The following year, Edward was posted to Ulster as a major in the Royal Scots Greys. Within three weeks he had been recalled. It was felt that as a cousin of the Queen he would be a potential target for the IRA. Edward was bitterly angry and upset, but despite his protests the decision had been made. From that moment on Edward began seriously to reconsider his career. If his Royal status was going to mean that he was treated differently from other soldiers, it was going to make it difficult for him to continue.

By now Katharine had overcome much of her earlier shyness and, since settling back in England, had began to take on the Royal duties that were expected of her. She had a number of high-profile roles, including Controller Commandant of the Women's Royal Army Corps, and she was the youngest-ever Chancellor of Leeds University. Katharine often found herself representing the Queen at functions that her Royal cousin was unable to attend.

Royal duties are arduous, requiring much preparation, and are often gruelling: hours of standing around, shaking hands, making polite conversation. Katharine describes herself as being 'not very robust', but she never let tiredness or lack of enthusiasm show. She was always polite and charming. With her quiet manner and

Edward Wing/Camera Press

ready smile, she rapidly became a very popular choice of Royal guest in her own right.

With these duties went engagements that often took her away from home. Katharine did what was expected of her conscientiously, but her heart was always at home with her children, and she tried to arrange matters so that she rarely spent nights away from them. She had a right to be proud of the way that she was bringing up her children. They were turning out to be bright and well-adjusted, and although George, after his display of exuberance at the Sooty show, had turned out to be far more sensitive and reserved than had been expected initially, he was already showing signs of being strikingly intelligent.

In 1973 Katharine's father, Sir William Worsley, died. She was left £100,000 in his will. When Marina had died, five years previously, she

♚Above *In the 'sixties and early 'seventies Katharine was often to be seen pushing a pram through the streets of Iver. She has always made it clear that, of her many roles, those of wife and mother are the most important*

♚*Meanwhile, Edward was pursuing his career in the Army. However, after he had spent just three weeks in Belfast in February 1971, the powers that be decided that a member of the Royal Family must not be exposed to the dangers of active service in Northern Ireland and a furious Duke was forced to depart for Scotland* right

♚*Katharine* below *combined two of her interests when, as Chancellor of Leeds University, she opened a nursery for the children of students and staff*

PA/Topham

had left only £17,398, once punitive death duties had been paid. So the Kents had now received all the money they could expect to inherit. They were receiving some money from the Civil List, but not enough to make a material difference. They were forced to acknowledge that the growing demands of a young family, and the expenses of living at Coppins, were becoming impossible to support. By 1974 they knew that they had no choice but to sell Coppins and buy a smaller property somewhere else.

Two new homes

With the money they made from the sale they bought Anmer Hall, a six-bedroom house standing in 10 acres in the village of Anmer, part of the Sandringham estate. The Queen also offered them York House in St James's Palace, which they use as their London base.

PA/Topham

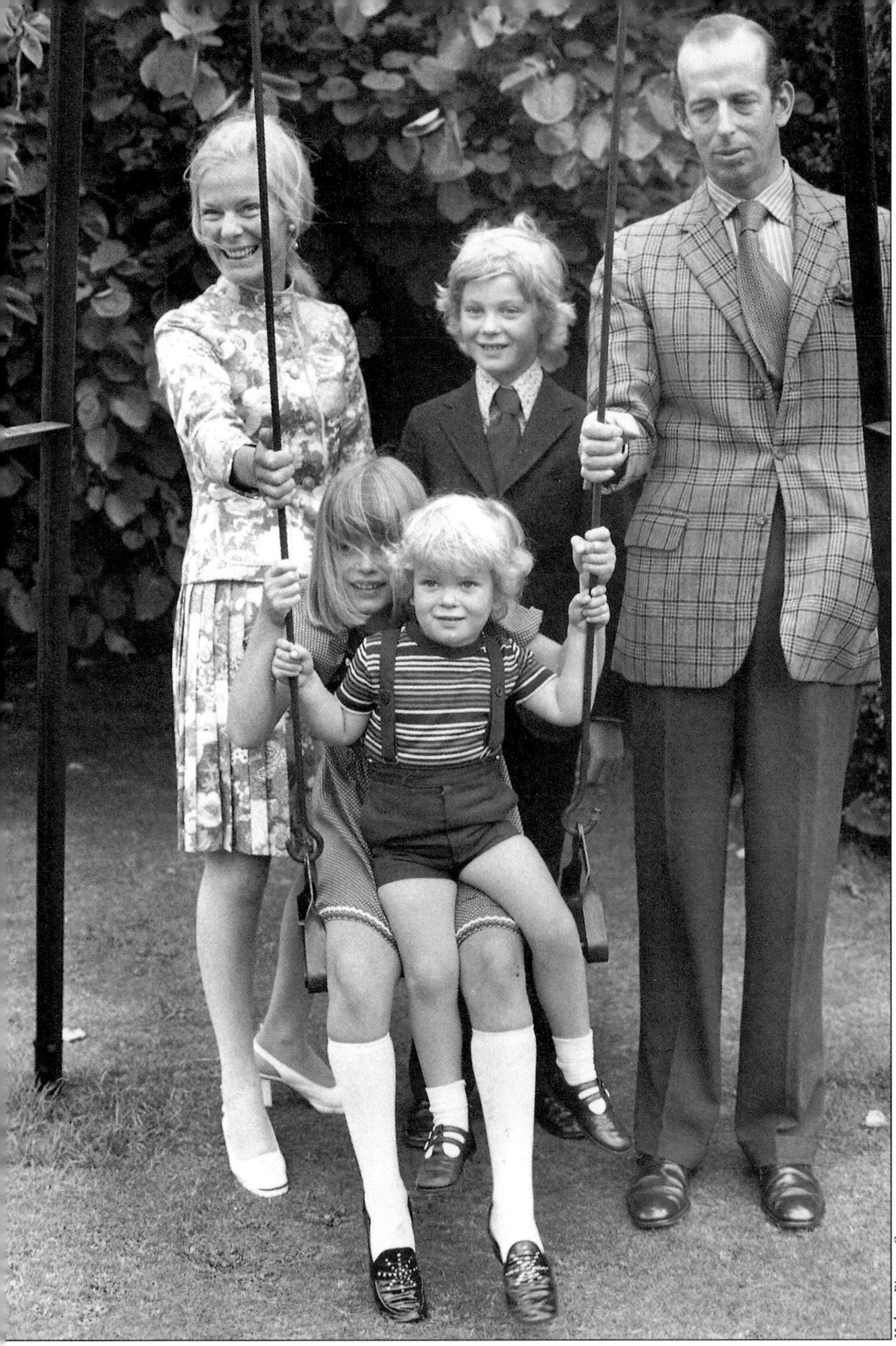

the fourth time, at the rather late age of 44. They were both thrilled at the prospect, but Katharine especially. She loved children, particularly babies, and her little family was now growing up. Nicholas, the 'baby', was already six, Helen was 12, and George was a teenager of 14.

By October Katharine was five months pregnant. On 4 October she started to feel unwell, and so seriously did Edward take this that he came back early from a working trip to Iran. It was soon clear that something was wrong. That evening Edward drove her himself to the King Edward VII Hospital for Officers in London.

> ### 'Human life is sacred and uniquely valuable. It is a gift of God and, as such, must never be taken for granted'
>
> KATHARINE

The team of doctors who attended the Duchess included the Queen's own gynaecologist, George Pinker. But all their expertise could not save the baby. By the evening of 5 October it was all over. Dr Donald Coggan, the Archbishop of Canterbury and a close friend of Katharine's, arrived at the hospital to give her comfort and stayed for half an hour. But no one, not even a loving husband, can give any true comfort to a mother who has lost her last-chance baby, and for Katharine this was the start of a long period of great unhappiness.

Hulton Picture Company

There had been a further pressure to sell Coppins, which had nothing to do with finances. It had been pronounced a security risk. Scotland Yard said that 'it would take a small army to give a place like Coppins complete protection because it is too exposed'.

Royal considerations and security had curtailed Edward's army career; lack of finances and security had lost him his family home. It now seemed time to learn the lessons from this. Edward decided to leave the Army and to make his career in something that would bring in more money and where his Royal birth would be a plus, rather than a minus. In 1976 he accepted the position of vice-chairman of the British Overseas Trade Board.

This new job eased the financial pressures, and in June 1977 there was further happy and unexpected news. Katharine was pregnant for

♛**Above** *Edward, Katharine and the children in the grounds of their new country home Anmer Hall, into which they had just moved. Katharine, who had gone on record as saying 'I'd love a large family,' was loath to think that there would be no more babies. In 1977, she was thrilled to discover that she was expecting her fourth child. But it was not to be. Newspaper headlines on 6 October* right *trumpeted a very private tragedy to the world*

John Frost Historical Newspapers

WELL-EARNED HAPPINESS

For all their devotion to public duties, the Kents have had a rich and enjoyable family life with many moments of shared happiness over the last 30 years. Journeys abroad have often taken the Duke and Duchess away from their family, but bonds between the children and parents have stood the test well. Although the Duke's mother was initially opposed to their match, her memory is still revered

👑The Second Duke prepares to take over the duties of his beloved father, whose portrait hangs on the wall behind him *right*. This official photograph was taken at Coppins just before the young Duke flew to Singapore with his mother, who in 1952 went on a tour of the Far East as official representative of the Crown

👑An official wedding group at Hovingham Hall *below* taken after the ceremony at York Minster. The best man is Edward's brother, Prince Michael of Kent. Standing behind the four smaller bridesmaids on the right is the familiar figure of Princess Anne, while Willa Worsley, Katharine's niece, is the little girl closest to the bride

♛The move from Coppins to Anmer Hall *above* was something of a trauma for the Kents, but they soon learned to appreciate the advantages of their splendid new house. Nicholas already seems quite at home at Anmer, as he enjoys clambering into the birdbath

♛In January 1964 the Duke represented his regiment in the Army Ski Championships at St Moritz, but took time off from training with Katharine *below*. At the time she was pregnant with her second child, Helen, who would be born in April

♛Katharine's sapphire and diamond engagement ring *above* remains a symbol of that blissful moment for which the young couple were forced to wait so long. When Edward's parents had got engaged 26 years before, George had given Marina a very similar square sapphire flanked by diamonds. Until recently sapphires have been the favourite stone for Royal engagement rings

As a child, Lady Helen Windsor was not a girl to fade quietly into the background. Feeling left out at her elder brother's sports day *below* the three-year-old Helen organizes a high-jump competition of her own

Jack Esten/Camera Press

Norman Parkinson/Camera Press

♛In this charming Norman Parkinson portrait of the Kents' children taken in 1975 *left*, the youngest, Nicholas, is flanked by Helen and George. The picture is a fine study of the contrasting personalities of the three children

♛The Earl of St Andrews starts his apprenticeship as a member of the Royal Family *above*. Aged three, he was a kilted page at the wedding of Fiona Bowes-Lyon, daughter of a cousin of the Queen Mother, at the Brompton Oratory in 1966

Hulton Picture Company

Edward Wing/Camera Press

♛Nicholas, despite a fine set of Fauntleroy curls, lets the side down on one of his first public appearances. An indulgent nanny does her best to quieten his sobs

♛George, aged seven, attracted a lot of silly comment from the popular press when he revealed a taste for hot dogs during the Badminton Horse Trials

Popperfoto

PA/Topham

♛ *The Duchess of Kent arrived on the steps of King Edward VII Hospital in London above, on 26 April 1978, to undergo a gall bladder operation the following day. The illness left her extremely weak for many weeks afterwards*

LIFE OF COMPASSION

THROUGH HER OWN EXPERIENCE OF ILL-HEALTH AND DEPRESSION, KATHARINE DEVELOPED AN ACUTE SENSIBILITY TO ALL HUMAN SUFFERING. HER WARM NATURE ENDEARS HER – BOTH IN PUBLIC AND IN PRIVATE – TO EVERYONE SHE MEETS

WITHIN DAYS THE DUCHESS WAS OUT OF hospital, and the doctors predicted a full recovery. She was home in time for her husband's birthday party, which they celebrated at York House. She had been photographed on the steps of the hospital, looking pale but smiling, offering her 'warm thanks' for the sympathy that she had received, 'which has helped me a great deal'.

It seemed that Katharine had indeed made a complete recovery. She was seen in public again just three weeks after the miscarriage, on 27 October, at the Silver Jubilee Fashion Spectacular at the New London Theatre. She was in her usual form the next month, when, as Commander-in-Chief, she visited the Women's Royal Army College in Camberley, Surrey, on 27 November.

Over the next few months she made a number of official visits, serene, smiling and, although quieter, no quieter than usual.

But although on the surface everything seemed to be fine, the emotional impact of losing her baby was yet to be truly felt. By acting as if everything were normal, Katharine hoped to make it so, but rushing back into work just postponed the moment of grief.

By early 1978 Edward was beginning to realize that Katharine had been much more marked by the events in October than she had let on. The outward veneer of calm and gaiety was beginning to crack. She began to cancel engagements at short notice, even leaving early from an official visit to a production of Wagner's *Das Rheingold* in Manchester.

♛ *Music and singing proved to be a great source of pleasure and comfort to Katharine and helped to pull her out of her depression. In 1978, she was accepted into the Bach Choir which she still sings with today. The Duchess is seen right during a performance of Berlioz's Requiem at the Royal Albert Hall, London*

♛ *Norman Parkinson's portrait of the Duke and Duchess far right, first published in 1985, does full justice to the couple's stately presence*

Alan Davidson/Camera Press

Hulton Picture Company

the better, and the family hoped that now she would start to recover.

But life was to deal her another blow. In January 1979 her mother, Lady Worsley, died. The death of a parent is always hard, but the death of the last surviving parent is hardest. It is a time when people confront their own mortality, feel that they are 'next in line'. Psychologically and emotionally this could not have come at a worse time for Katharine, struggling, as she already was, with the grief of losing a child and the knowledge that age was against her and she had no chance of having another.

Her mother's death plunged her into the deepest depression yet – so bad that within two months it was clear that hospitalization was the only answer. The official story was that she had

PA/Topham

Physically Katharine was not standing up so well either. On 26 April she was admitted to hospital for a gall bladder operation, and when this was over she was considered too ill to look after herself. The Queen invited her to Windsor to recuperate under her care.

Now Katharine, and all her family, realized that there was more to getting better than putting a brave face on it. The depressions came more often and more severely and sometimes without warning. The erstwhile conscientious and dutiful Duchess often had to cancel engagements at the last minute when she anticipated that, once again, she would not be able to cope.

Music therapy

It was to music Edward looked in his attempt to help his wife get better. He encouraged her to try for a place in the Bach Choir. Katharine had a lovely soprano voice which she rarely used, and singing in a famous choir seemed to be an ideal tonic. In October 1978 Katharine took a voice test and was accepted into the choir. For a while this really seemed to have affected her spirits for

♔Above *As the Kent family leaves St Paul's Cathedral after a service for the Queen Mother's 80th birthday, the Duchess lends a listening ear to her youngest son, Nicholas. However official the occasion, Katharine will not let it interfere with the warm and close relationship she enjoys with her children*

♔*Not just a handshake but a royal hug as well above right – schoolboy Andrew is one of the many handicapped children who benefited from the three Sunshine Coaches for outdoor activities, whose keys the Duchess of Kent handed over to the Variety Club of Great Britain at St James's Palace on 24 May 1982*

been admitted to the Edward VII hospital for a period of 'supervised rest' and that she was suffering from 'nervous strain'.

In truth she had suffered a nervous breakdown. Katharine spent nearly seven weeks in hospital, allowed only to see her husband, children and very close relatives.

When Katharine was released from hospital she was very much better, though physically she was less strong than she had ever been. The profound losses that she had suffered were to leave their mark for even longer. For the next eight years Katharine continued to suffer on and off from depressions.

For Katharine almost the worst thing about her depressions was that for periods she could not be the kind of mother she wanted to be for her children. It was her eldest and most sensitive child, George, who seemed to suffer most. He had shown signs of an exceptional intelligence from the age of 12, when he competed against 76 other candidates for 15 Eton scholarships. He was the first ever member of the Royal Family to become a King's Scholar at Eton since the scholarships were founded in the 15th century.

Failed exams

But 1979, the year of his mother's breakdown, saw him sitting his 'A' Levels. It was impossible for him to put his worry about his mother out of his mind, and when the results came through he had failed two out of his three subjects. But he had grit and determination, and he sat the exams again a few months later. This time he passed all the exams with top grades, and the school predicted that he most certainly had a brilliant future in front of him.

In 1983 Katharine was again admitted to hospital, this time for an operation to remove an ovarian cyst. This operation left her very weak, and she had to rest for several months. The

Hulton Picture Company

🔶 *A lot of the Duchess's charity work is devoted to Age Concern, and she admits to having a soft spot for the elderly. She is seen above with Bruce Forsyth on the TV show* Play Your Cards Right *which won the charity a brand-new minibus*

🔶 *'The Lady from Wimbledon', as Katharine is often referred to, presents John McEnroe with the Men's Singles Final Cup in 1984 left. An avid spectator of the sport, she also plays tennis herself about once a week*

Hulton Picture Company

press, now alerted to the fact that the Duchess had suffered from depression, stated that she had suffered from a breakdown, resulting in one of the rare denials from Buckingham Palace.

Helen seemed to take her mother's illness more in her stride. Unlike George, she was no academic. She did not particularly distinguish herself at any of the schools she attended, and her 'A' Level results were not good enough to get her a place at university. By the time her mother was admitted to hospital for the operation on her ovaries, Helen, aged 19, had left home and was sharing a small flat with a friend.

With the two older children growing up York House seemed very empty. Helen had her own flat and George, who had spent time in

THE HOSPICE VISITOR

Nowhere has the Duchess of Kent's compassion been more evident than as a visitor to hospices, the hospitals for the dying. She has been particularly moved by the children she has met in these places, and in 1983 she opened Helen House, a hospice specially for dying children. Before she went there she didn't know whether she would be able to cope. 'I've been to so many hospices,' she said, 'but this is my first children's one and it is so important. I don't really know how it will affect me.' But she found the experience so profound that she became a frequent visitor

Oxford & County Newspapers

Jim Bennett/Alpha

India working for the Save the Children Fund, was now at Cambridge reading history. It was decided, therefore, to keep Nicholas at home and, instead of sending him to Eton, enrol him at Westminster as a day boy. During the months of Katharine's recuperation from illness it was a comfort to have him at home with her.

After a complete rest, Katharine felt strong enough to resume normal life again. And this time things really did seem to be different. Something had lifted inside her. She was able to enjoy life again, and she looked with new appreciation on her family, who had stood by her so steadfastly – her husband in particular.

A complete recovery

From that time onwards, the Duchess of Kent has never really looked back. She is still one of the more retiring Royals and she will never enjoy the blooming health of some of her relatives, but she works hard and has earned that over-used royal adjective 'gracious'. What she brings to her work is the special empathy and compassion of one who has really suffered herself. She has many official titles and duties, but it is notable that the organizations that are closest to her heart are those that deal with people who are suffering in some way.

For instance, the Duchess is a Samaritan, and took their training course when she became their patron. There was a time when she, too, took calls from the desperate and lonely. 'The course taught me an enormous amount about life,' she has said. 'If you spend quite a few months talking to people who are suicidal, mostly through loneliness, you do begin to

The year 1988 was marked by the arrival of two 'additions' to the Kent family. On 9 January, Sylvana Tomaselli became the wife of the Earl of St Andrews, above, and in December of the same year Katharine's new daughter-in-law gave birth to a son and heir: Edward George, who was given the courtesy title Baron Downpatrick right

'**Some people are naturals; some need to learn warmth. The Duchess is a natural'**

THE GENERAL SECRETARY OF
THE SAMARITANS

PA/Topham

understand people and their problems...'

The Duchess is also a regular visitor to hospices where she gives comfort to the dying. 'I never have to think about what I should say because they, the ones who are ill, are the ones who give you the confidence to talk to them,' she has said. 'That's the most remarkable part of hospice work. They give much more to you than you could ever give to them.'

As her health has returned, so she has become more confident, and she and her husband entertain more than they did in the early years. They too now find themselves attracted to the artistic and famous, particularly in the music world. Katharine says she grew to love opera after hearing Placido Domingo sing, and she went on to form a warm friendship with him. George Solti also became a friend, as did Jacqueline du Pré, whose brilliant career was, tragically, cut short by multiple sclerosis. It is absolutely in character that the Duchess contiued to visit Jacqueline du Pré as her illness worsened, and she says that she feels lucky that she was 'able to be with her just a few hours before she died'.

LADY HELEN WINDSOR

By rights the daughter of the Duke and Duchess of Kent should have been able to live her life discreetly unnoticed, as there are plenty more senior Royals to get the attention. But unluckily for her she is also one of the most strikingly good-looking of the Royal females, and her fun-loving escapades have also captured press attention. It was the press that first reported (or invented) her nickname of 'Melons', which has constantly irritated her.

In 1984, when she started work at Christie's Auctioneers, she hoped that she might lose her party girl image: 'It is my first serious job. And I want to make my career working in contemporary art...' she said. 'I want to have a serious career...'

Mark Stewart/Camera Press

The Bach Choir, which she joined just before her mother's death, was eventually able to give the Duchess the comfort and pleasure that Edward had envisaged. She still sings with it, but like all the other choristers, has to re-audition every three years. 'It's a nightmare,' she says. 'We all hate it. We sing harmonies and unaccompanied pieces. Everybody has a cold or sore throat when they appear before the musical director. It's terrifying. I'd rather make a speech than do that.'

For someone who is not very sporty herself, spectator sport is her passion. Not that she

♛ *The present home of the Duke and Duchess of Kent, Croker End House below, is situated near Henley-on-Thames in Oxfordshire. The former vicarage with its charming, cosy atmosphere provides the setting for many a family gathering*

♛ *As a day pupil at Westminster Lord Nicholas Windsor above saw more of his parents during his adolescent years than his brother or sister did. His lively and enthusiastic nature brought comfort and hope to Katharine when she was suffering from depression. But in 1988 the much-loved 'baby' of the family briefly turned into the* bête noir *when he hit the headlines after having been found in possession of cannabis in St James's Park*

Glenn Harvey

Rex Features

doesn't take part: she likes windsurfing but, by her own admission, is 'not very good at it', she bicycles a bit, she says, plays tennis once a week and dances a little. Following in the footsteps of Princess Marina, Katharine is closely associated with Wimbledon. She says that for three or four weeks after the tournament she cannot move around London without being surrounded by Americans pointing her out as 'the lady from Wimbledon'.

The Duchess's twin loves of music and sport are shared with her husband. He is president of both the Football Association and the All England Lawn Tennis and Croquet Club, among his many patronages.

But their family remains their chief joy, even now that the children are grown up. They have

'We may not have long but we can live each moment intensely'

KATHARINE

given them more freedom than is usual in the Royal Family, and the pay-off has been that their children remain close to them. They did not raise objections to George's romance with a Catholic divorcée who was older than himself; neither have they tried to check the youthful high spirits of Helen. When Helen was photographed smoking and drinking in public at the age of 18, they decided that it was wiser not to make a fuss and rely on her essential good sense to win through in the end.

Ordinary people

The Duke and Duchess of Kent think of themselves as quite ordinary people. The Duchess seems oblivious to the fact that her sensitivity towards the ill and dying is something special. 'I don't believe there is anyone in the world who hasn't suffered something,' she once said. 'All of us have had some cross to bear and it is through these experiences that one learns empathy and compassion.'

It is enlightening, and not surprising, that the Worsley family motto which Katharine was brought up with says, 'Do good to as many persons as possible.'

♛ *A radiant Katharine* left *arrives at the Odeon, Leicester Square, for the première of the cartoon film* Little Mermaid *in October 1990. As her health has returned, she and her husband enjoy going out and entertaining more than in previous years*